NEW YORK'S

City Streets

NEW YORK'S

City Streets

A GUIDE TO MAKING YOUR BLOCK MORE LIVELY

AND MORE LIVABLE

BY MARY GROZIER AND RICHARD ROBERTS

THE COUNCIL ON THE ENVIRONMENT OF NEW YORK CITY

Typography and cover design by Hermann Strohbach

Single copies $1.25

The Council on the Environment of New York City
Room 228
51 Chambers Street
New York, New York 10007

Bulk copies available.
Call (212) 566-0990 or
write to the Council

Acknowledgments

Robert Alpern • Michael Altschuler • A.N.O. Building Supply Co., Inc. • Brooke Astor • Bedford Stuyvesant Restoration Corporation • Barry Benepe • Robert Benjamin, Inc. • Sheila Berkley • Joan Buck • Betsy Busch • Phyllis Cerf • Children's Aid Society, East Harlem Center • City Walls, Inc. • City Art Commission • Cityarts Workshop, Inc. • The City of New York Department of City Planning • The City of New York Department of Highways • The City of New York Department of Public Works • The City of New York Department of Traffic • The City of New York Environmental Protection Administration • The City of New York Housing and Development Administration • The City of New York Office of Midtown Planning and Development • The City of New York Office of Neighborhood Government • The City of New York Parks, Recreation and Cultural Affairs Administration • The City of New York Transportation Administration • Nadine Daskiloff • Sophie Dolgin • Diana Douglas • Edison Electric Institute • Entwisle Corporation • Environmental Action Coalition • Ann Ferebee • The Festival Company • Barie-Fez-Barrington • Doris Freedman • M. Paul Freidberg • Gregory Gallina • Percival Goodman • Mac Gordon • Dorothy Greene • Oliver Hamill • Hastings Paving Company, Inc. • William Hodgson • Anna and Paul Gray Hoffman • Holophane Company, Inc. • Norma Holt • Interboro Surface Company • William Joseph • Mary Jane Kantor • Leslie Kramer • Robert Lieberman • Terrie LoCicero • Londino Stone Company • Anita Margill • Judy Marshall • Maybrick, Inc. • McGraw Edison Co. • Mellor Gym Supply Corp. • Minolta Corporation • Museum of the City of New York • National Electrical Manufacturers Ass'n. • Neidermeyer-Martin Co. (Timberform Division) • New York Botanical Gardens • New York Horticultural Society • New York Public Library • Joyce Nye • The Parks Council • Mel Pekarsky • Aurora Perisi • Pfaff and Kendall • Playground Corporation of America • Professional Children's School, Inc. • Project Two • Donald Richardson • Bernard Rothzeid • Salsich Recreation Incorporated • Salute to the Seasons Fund for a More Beautiful New York • Raymond Sanchez • Joyce Selig • Amit Sikdar • Arlene Simon • Spring City Electrical Mfg., Inc. • State Supply Co., Inc. • Richard Stein • Street and Highways Safety Lighting Bureau • Unimark Corp. • Vollmar Associates • William H. Whyte • Marilyn Wood • Neila Wyman.

A special thanks is due Random House, whose help and public-spirited generosity helped to turn an idea into reality.

Contents AND HOW TO USE THEM

1 • Introduction

Some critics say the city is dangerous to live in and impossible to govern and has outlived its time. Is it true? Or is the city still an exciting place where neighbors can get together to take advantage of the opportunities it offers?

page 1

2 • The Council on the Environment

This book was written as an answer for people who came to the Council on the Environment with questions about how they could make their blocks better places on which to live. What is the Council? What does it do? Who are the men and women on the Council?

page 5

3 • Getting started

The best way to improve your neighborhood is by means of a block association. If there is none on your block, start one. Here's how—how to make contacts, set up meetings, choose leaders, assign jobs, get publicity.

page 9

4 • Taking the pulse of your block

Before you can improve your block you have to know what's needed, and to do that you have to ask questions. Here are the kinds of questions to ask: about sanitation, lighting, utilities, about how the street is used and who uses it, about how your neighbors feel about the block and what they'd like to see done.

page 17

5 • What are the options?

There are basically six ways to make your block more beautiful, more comfortable, more livable.

You can close the street temporarily for fairs, festivals or other events...   page 28
...by making it a play street...   page 31
...or a school street   page 36
You can decorate it with fabrics, paint or materials   page 36
You can put furnishings (such as baskets, benches, bicycle racks or play equipment) in the right kind of places   page 45
You can plant shrubs, trees or flowers   page 52
You can use lights and paving   page 58
Or you can convert abandoned lots into parks or play areas   page 61

6 • Maintaining the momentum

Don't let your project bog down. Keep it moving. Here's how to keep a record of your progress, to know where you stand, what still has to be done, what permits you have to get, what money you might need to raise. And where to turn for assistance.   page 65

7 • Finding the funds

This can be crucial. Although some projects cost little, you may find yourself getting more ambitious, and turning to programs that *do* need money. Where can you get it? Well, there are local sources of course.   page 69
And then there's big money, which is available from foundations and the like. But to get that kind of money, you have to make the right kind of approach. Here's how.   page 71

Appendices

The questionnaire: A simple questionnaire that can be used to help you take the pulse of the block. Arranged so that you can Xerox it right from the book and distribute the copies to your neighbors.
                                              page 75

Who-where: An alphabetical list of agencies, offices, commissions and the like, together with an assortment of topics—also arranged alphabetically—that are likely to crop up, such as "abandoned car removal," "barbecues on the street," "entertainment," "permits," etc.
                                              page 79

"One of the things we learned was to do things together."

"The whole block is a lot more peaceful. People grew to . . . well, feel a lot warmer to each other."

"We found out it's really true that the squeaky wheel gets the grease."

How one block was reborn

"The outsiders—the characters who used to hang around —they're gone."

"It's wonderful!"

The people on East Seventh Street have a lot to say, but that's because there's a lot for them to talk about.

East Seventh between Avenue C and Avenue D is no heaven on earth. It doesn't look too much different from the blocks around it. A little brighter maybe, with planters on window sills and fresh paint on some doors and stoops and in hallways. The sidewalks are cleaner and the garbage pails are lined up more neatly against the buildings. But that's because Charlie Johnson gets up at some ungodly hour every day to sweep and straighten. The people on the block pay Charlie for the service but maybe Charlie would do it without pay—if he could—because, like the others on the block, Charlie feels that Seventh between C and D is something special.

It's home.

The flower pots and the fresh paint and the mural on the wall next to what used to be a vacant lot and is now a playground— all these things count. But what counts more than anything is something you can't see. It's the spirit, the feeling.

Three years ago Seventh was a typical Lower East Side block. It had been sliding downhill for years, with the litter getting a little worse all the time and the junkies and hoods hanging around.

"Then," says Betty Carol Seller—everyone on the block calls her "B.C.," the block association "came back to life."

"There had been an association earlier," B.C. says, "but it was focused on owners. This time people began to talk to each other. One man was the block activist. We got sort of a community forum going, started meeting together."

Eddie Salter, a black artist, was in the thick of it.

"People were concerned for safety," he says. "We wanted to at least develop a piece of land for kids to play in."

The newly reborn block association focused on a vacant lot. A real eyesore strewn with burned-out mattresses, broken glass, bricks and rubble.

There was a block party—a huge success (the people on Seventh still talk about it)—at which people chipped in with money, ideas. One man contributed a load of plants. That was in June of '72. The association by then had picked up speed and support. The block party really shot it forward.

Preparing for that party took a lot of work. The games, the prizes, the food, the music, decorations and exhibits, the clean-ups and the arrangements for permits—all these things took time and thought and energy. People got together to decide on the details, then worked together to carry out the plans.

And they stayed together.

Since the party, the people of Seventh Street have been getting together from time to time for clean-ups. When it's a big one (like tackling a vacant lot) they borrow rakes and shovels from the Park Department, and get help from the Sanitation Department. They've learned whom to call to get results.

Since the party, the people of Seventh Street have been sharing responsibility for taking the younger kids on field trips around the city.

Since the party, the people of Seventh Street have been working together to solicit contributions for a new project: acquiring another vacant lot so it can be turned into a basketball court.

As Eddie Salter says: "It's one of the few streets in this area that has people working the way they do. They're doing it out of mutual concern."

"We were lucky," says B.C., speaking of the block party, the changes that it brought and the playground it led to. "We won the Molly Parnis prize and used the money to buy playground equipment."

And Rose Doctor, who runs the little candy store near Avenue D, likes to talk about how.

everyone on the block—white, black, Puerto Ricans, Jews, young and old—worked to clean things up and how it affected people's lives.

"You know," she says, "people got to sitting outside again, using the block like a living room."

Seventh between C and D. Not just another block. It's home.

1 • Introduction

The city is under attack.

Not for the first time, and not for the last, its critics are saying it is living on borrowed time. It is, those critics say, like a dinosaur—too big, too clumsy, and impossible to govern. And, like a dinosaur, it will soon be extinct, replaced by some higher form.

Or so they say.

Traffic jams make commerce almost impossible (or at least unprofitable) and businessmen are fleeing to the open spaces. Filthy air makes breathing unhealthy and filthy streets make sightseeing unappealing. Crime and the fear of crime keep visitors away and drive the affluent to the suburbs and beyond. Parks are unsafe because of muggers and unattractive because of vandals. The more you try to solve the problems, the worse they become. There is no hope. The city is dead and is only waiting around to be buried.

Or so they say.

But it isn't so.

Of course there are problems. Traffic jams do waste time, money and gasoline. But businessmen aren't fleeing the city like flocks of migrating birds. Crime and the fear of crime do keep visitors away (but only some) and do drive the affluent to the suburbs and beyond (but only some).

Yes—everything the critics say is true. But only a little bit true.

There are muggers and filthy air and dirty streets. But not as many and not as much and not as bad. And for every minus the critics think up there is a plus they forget about. For every grim word they use—like dangerous, dirty or noisy—there is a word they overlook. Like exciting, stimulating, convenient.

The city, in short, in spite of its drawbacks, is a great place to live.

That doesn't mean it can't be made even better. The government

1

is trying to make it better, the experts are trying. But basically, it's up to the people. When they try, it really counts, because making the city better from the bottom up—instead of from the top down—gets right to the heart of it all.

One way that people can make city life better is by making greater use of one of those things the city has less of than the suburbs or rural areas—space. Foot for foot, acre for acre, city space is more heavily used than space elsewhere. Its space is crowded with buildings, with heavily trafficked streets, with people.

This book is meant to help you use space to its fullest, to help you improve your city from the bottom up, where it really counts. This book is meant to help you do things on your own block. It will show you how to investigate new and creative ways to change your streetscape so that it will become more inviting, so that you and your neighbors will find new enjoyment and relaxation in using your street.

It's meant to tell you how to get around or cut through the red tape that can stall or stop a project, that can keep you from putting benches on your block or making it brighter with paint or lights or trees. It's meant to tell you where to turn for guidance, for help, for money, where to go for permits and applications. It's meant to help you get things done on your own, but also to tell you where you can find help when it's needed. It names people and places and agencies.

The book's message is spread throughout its pages. In the pictures that show you how things can look (when they're done with enthusiasm and confidence and know-how). In the advice and hints and lists. In the warnings.

If that message had to be condensed somehow, summed up and put down in one boiled-down paragraph, perhaps that paragraph would read this way:

By being organized, by being vocal and active and alert, by being aware of opportunities and willing and able to take advantage of them, you and your neighbors can change the face of the city. In a city as big as New York we sometimes lose heart, we wonder if there really is a way to break through the old patterns and to raise spirits somehow. The answer is a resounding "yes!"

The men and women at the Council on the Environment hope that that message comes across loud and clear in the pages that follow. They hope that this handbook will encourage you and your neighbors to meet the challenge of that message and to join in working for a new vision of the city.

2 • The Council on the Environment

This book came into being in response to people. How, people asked the Council on the Environment, can we make our block a better place to live on? How can we make it more comfortable, more attractive?

People, individually and in organized groups, speaking for themselves alone or for their neighbors as well, wrote to the Council, phoned it, dropped in at its offices to ask for help and guidance.

This book is the answer. It is the Council's way of saying that under-used, neglected streets—streets that are no more than routes to and from home—strike at the very heart of community life. Such streets are cemeteries where the hopes and potential for social interaction are buried.

The answers this book offers evolved from meetings between members of the Council staff and community groups and individuals, plus research. No one at the Council pretends to have all the answers or feels that the answers are in any sense final. Ideas change, people change, the city changes. And as these changes come, the answers in this book will become less accurate.

But the main ideas, the guidelines, the principles—and these are a vital part of the book—will remain basically valid.

Although the Council is a relative newcomer to the urban scene, this book is not its first venture into publishing.

In 1971, a year after it was established by Mayor John V. Lindsay and Marian S. Heiskell, the Council published "Birds today. People tomorrow?" a pamphlet that has become something of a best-seller, with more than two and a half million copies distributed.

5

Its monthly newspaper, Our Daily Planet, reports on new laws affecting the urban environment, on challenges to old laws, on controversies and campaigns; it profiles environmental activists, reviews films and publications, offers plans and suggestions for better living, and prints the findings of its own original investigative reporting.

(Your contributions to Our Daily Planet will be welcomed. Is there environmental activity in your neighborhood that might be of interest to others? Do you know of a sanitation, sewage, air-pollution or related problem around the city that should be corrected? Do you know people who are doing interesting work that affects the urban scene? Turn your tip in by phoning 566-0990. Or write to the Planet at 51 Chambers Street, New York, N.Y. 10007.)

But the Council is more than a publisher. It promotes and originates research and demonstration projects. Its staff, its members and its volunteers were right in the middle of the effort by government, industry and citizen groups to come up with and press for the use of new kinds of refuse bags. The bags they helped to develop and promote have decreased litter by reducing spillage, have made life less noisy by eliminating the clanging of metal cans and have cut down on wasted time by eliminating the need for sanitationmen to make return trips to the curb with empty cans.

The people at the Council work with schools, industry, government agencies and ordinary citizens to create a new awareness of the environment and to do something to make New York City's environment a better one for everyone.

The Council is a broadly based citizens group within the Office of the Mayor. Its funds come entirely from contributions by individuals and organizations. It has a dedicated, hard-working staff of men and women and 100 unsalaried members, including not only heads of city agencies, but also leaders and representatives of business, industry and labor and spokesmen for scientists, students, the professions and civic and neighborhood groups.

Those 100 members give their time, their energies and their counsel because they feel they are helping people to bring out the best in themselves, their neighbors and their city in a way that's visible and tangible and real. They are helping people who want to start by changing the face of the street they live on.

3 • Getting started

Before you can change the face of your street you must get to its heart—the people who live there, work there, play there—and you must do so in a way that can lead to organized, cooperative action. No project or program, from the modest placing of a poster to the ambitious redesigning of an entire block, can succeed without the support of those whose lives will be affected by that project or program.

There are many ways to reach the people on your street, but the object of this book is not to show you all the possibilities and then turn you loose to pick one; the object is to offer you the best of what others have learned through experience. And what others have learned is this: the firmest foundation upon which you can build a neighborhood program is a block association. A block association provides a focal point for enthusiasm, a vehicle through which neighbors can pool their time, their talents, their ideas.

If you already have a block association you know what it is, how it works and—if your association is a vital, going concern—what it can accomplish. If not, form one. That's the indispensable first step on the road to revitalizing your neighborhood.

Block associations have been around, in one form or another, probably as long as cities themselves. But here in New York they began sprouting in their present form only about a generation ago— just after World War II. They grew naturally, out of a need for a combination of neighborliness, cooperative action and human contact.

566●1550 OPERATION BETTER BLOCK

There are now somewhere between 6,000 and 8,000 block associations in the city. Most have as their "territory" one actual, physical block—a piece of the city bounded by four streets—though some associations spill over to take in a neighboring block. Some, especially those in neighborhoods of one- and two-family homes, resemble suburban homeowner organizations; others have an almost militant orientation. Some, such as those in densely populated high-rise areas, have large and shifting memberships; others have small and much more stable memberships.

But all have one thing in common: a core of men and women determined to make their home neighborhood a vital, vibrant, good place to live. If you are determined to do that, and if there is no block association in your neighborhood, you can become the core of that core. You can start an association, and your enthusiasm can be contagious.

Not long ago, one energetic woman on Staten Island roused her neighbors, organized a clean-up campaign, persuaded the owner of vacant property to deed it to the city and then got the city to build a swimming pool and park on the land. And a Brooklyn woman, armed only with energy and a desire to rid her neighborhood of junkies, prostitutes and gamblers, overcame the apathy of her neighbors and led them in what became a 'successful campaign to overhaul their block.

By themselves, those women might not have succeeded. Together with their neighbors they accomplished marvels. Your success, like theirs, will depend upon your involving as many people as you can and upon your keeping as many people as possible—even those who take no active part—informed.

"Operation Better Block," a city program that began in 1968, can provide you with help in getting a block association going. Its excellent handbook, "New Yorkers: Get Yourselves Together," offers step-by-step guidelines. A capsule description from that handbook tells you the basics:

You can begin your block association with only a few individuals who care about the block and want to improve it. The first steps to organize your block are:

- Contact a few families and set up an informal meeting in someone's home.

- Find a leader, a temporary chairman to get your group started. Choose a resident or local community leader who has experience in community organization.

- Form a temporary steering committee to organize your block association.

- Elect or appoint permanent officers as soon as you have a solid core of members. Officers can be changed often to involve more association members in active leadership.

- Make your meetings informative, interesting and entertaining to attract the interest of the whole block.

- Choose an attractive, comfortable meeting place on or near your block, such as a school, church, community center or large living room in a private home. People don't like to travel far.

- Publicize the meeting at least a week in advance.

- Meetings should be short—no more than 1½ hours for business. Remember, many people work and others want to be with their families. People get bored.

- Keep the discussion open to everyone. Don't let one group take over.

- Try to get group consensus on issues.

- Assign tasks to people who will carry them out.

- Meetings should lead to action. People won't come back unless they see something's being done.

- The more people who know about your meetings and the project, the better. Publicize your meetings and activities as much as possible.

There is more than one way to publicize your meetings and activities. Posters and notices, strategically placed in well-trafficked spots, help. Notices in community newspapers can get the message across (if your project is big enough, or unusual or controversial, you can even find publicity through larger newspapers—but you have to let the editors know what's going on). And the best publicity of all is word of mouth. Talk it up! Enthusiasm is a necessary ingredient, but it can't do the job alone.

In offering its guidelines, the Better Block handbook advises you to have your block association include the following officers:

- **President:** The leader of the group who runs all meetings and is generally responsible for seeing that the goals and purposes of the association are carried out.

- **Vice President:** The deputy to the president who presides at meetings when the president cannot attend.

- **Secretary:** The member who keeps the minutes of the meetings and records all business transactions.

- **Treasurer:** The member who keeps financial records, manages the association's bank account and presents monthly reports at meetings.

- **Committee chairmen:** Members appointed by the president or elected by the group for specific program areas.

Remember, in organizing your block association, that people who own property in your area should be kept informed about what's going on, about what is planned and what is being done—even if they don't participate. In many cases the consent of a property owner is vital.

If you would like help in organizing your block association, contact the Mayor's Office of Neighborhood Government (see the where-to-find-help directory in the back of the book). That office, which is, by the way, the parent agency of Operation Better Block, serves as an idea exchange center. It is a storehouse of information on what works and what doesn't, of what routes lead to success and which ones are dead-ends.

Organizing doesn't have to be all hard work and a grind. Some of it can actually be fun. Others have found, for example, that one of the best ways to get a block association going is with a block party (the Brooklyn woman mentioned earlier was one of those; she roused her neighbors' interest through a block party for children).

You'll find lots of useful information about running block parties in the first part of the chapter titled What Are the Options, which begins on page 27 . It may seem like putting carts before horses, but why not turn to that section now for some ideas about block parties? And then why not do some original research by attending as many block parties as you can? As we said, it doesn't all have to be a grind.

If you do hold a block party as part of your organizing work, try to get as much ground work as possible done at that party. Distribute questionnaires, interview your neighbors, line up volunteers.

Questionnaires? Volunteers? What's that all about?

Go on, please, to the next chapter.

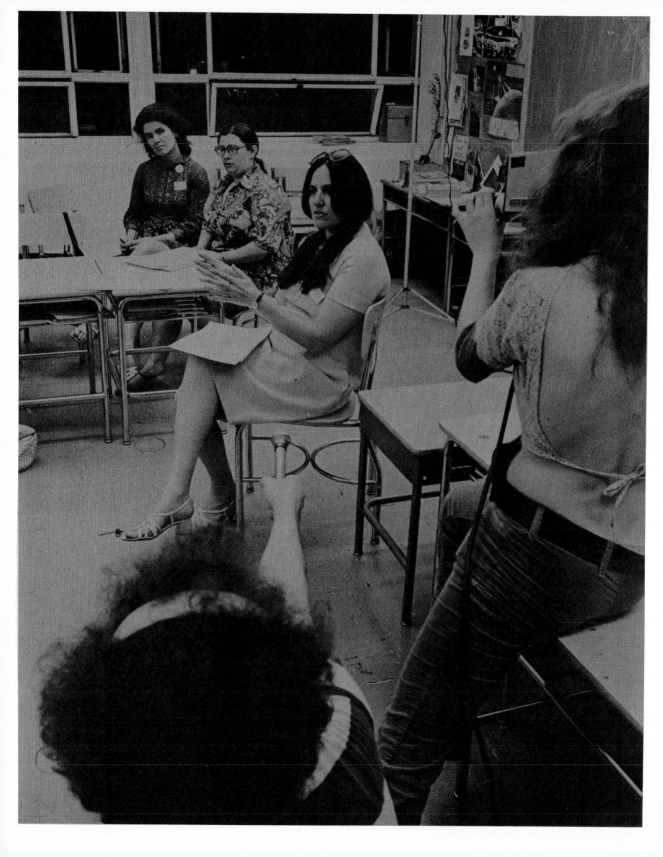

4 • Taking the pulse of your block

How much do you know about your block?

Do you know, for instance, how many people live on it? How many own property there, but live elsewhere? How many children there are? How many retired people? Do you know how wide your street is, how many hydrants there are—and where they are—how many street lights there are? Do you know how often garbage is collected? Where the gas lines and water mains are?

Do you know how your neighbors feel about the physical aspects of the block? What about services—how do they feel about santita-tion, for instance? About lighting? What kind of changes would they like to see?

These are the kinds of questions—these and many others—that have to be answered before you can make plans to change your block. For one thing, you cannot go somewhere (to a new, revital-ized block) without knowing where you are starting from (your present block). And for another, you cannot make plans without knowing how your neighbors feel about them.

Which brings us around to the questionnaires and the volunteers.

The questionnaire, which you will find at the back of the book, is designed to give you and your fellow block-association organizers a good idea of how many and what kind of people live, work or own property on your block. It should help you learn the kinds of changes, if any, others would like to see. Just as important, it will give you an idea of the kind of (and reasons for) opposition you are likely to run into.

As for the volunteers—whom you can recruit at a block party, through door-to-door appeals or at meetings—they are needed to answer questions about your block as it is now. They are the survey-takers, the observers, the crews of men, women and young people who will provide you with the information that is so essential to the formulation of any plans for change. Try to assign each volunteer, or team of volunteers, to one specific topic among the following:

Street housekeeping	What is the general state of cleanliness of the street? Where is litter most prevalent? What type of litter is most offensive and what is its source? How frequently is sanitation service provided? How effective is it? Who provides it? What are the hours of sanitation service? How frequently do residents, storekeepers or others provide supplementary cleaning of their homes, sidewalks or the street (hosing, sweeping, painting or other maintenance or repair)? How many residents use the street to walk their dogs? How many transients? Is there a stray-dog problem?
Street use	How many people use the street only to get to and from their homes or places of business? How many people use it for playing games? What are their ages? When do they play? How often? What do they play? How often do people socialize on the street? What are the most frequent hours for socializing? Where are the preferred spots? How many people socialize? Do people sun themselves, or sit outside? How many? How often? At what time of day? Where? What is the age-range breakdown of those who use the street? What percentage is pre-schoolers? Pre-teens? Teen-agers? etc. Is one side of the street used more often than the other by one age group? Are there times of the day preferred by each age group?
Children on the street	Do children from the block use the street for play? Do children from neighboring streets use it? What sort of things do the children play with? Toys? Games? Objects in the street? Does their playing disturb you or your neighbors?

Weather factors	What is the sunniest part of the street in the morning, the afternoon, the late afternoon? Is there a windy section? A protected section? A shady one or drafty one? Is the street—at the time of the survey—uncomfortably warm or cold?
Sound	Is the street noisy? What are the principal sources of noise and where are the noisiest spots? What hours are the noisiest? The quietest? Have you or your neighbors ever complained about noise? To whom? When? Did you get any results?
Trees, flowers and other growing things	What trees, plants, vines, planters, window boxes, gardens, etc., face or are on the street? Who owns or cares for them? What condition are they in?
Measurement and maintenance	How wide is the street from curb to curb? How wide are the sidewalks? In what condition is the street? The sidewalk? The curb? Where are the worst spots? What's the cause of the trouble? Do the stoops jut out and leave little room to pass? Are there other obstructions for pedestrians?
Lighting	How many lights does the street have? Can you see clearly along the entire length of the block at night? Are there pockets of shadow? Where? Are sidewalks and street equally well lighted? Are some spots on street or sidewalk better lighted than others? Is the lighting equipment in good repair? How many lights don't work? How many buildings have supplementary lighting on walls, stoops, in entranceways, elsewhere? Where are the supplementary lights? Are they well maintained? By whom?

Utilities	Electricity: In all boroughs, except the Fifth Ward in Queens, which is served by the Long Island Lighting Company, check with Consolidated Edison for the location of surface and sub-surface power lines, transformers and other equipment.

Gas: For the location of gas lines and other equipment check with Con Edison in Manhattan, the Bronx and parts of Queens (the Fifth Ward in Queens is served by LILCO) and with Brooklyn Union Gas Company in Brooklyn, Staten Island and some parts of Queens.

Water: Check with the Department of Water Resources for the location of mains and connectors.

Sewers: Locate and map the surface openings on your block. For the location of subsurface lines and other facilities consult the maps in your Borough Hall.

Police and fire communications equipment: These phones lines are maintained by the Empire City Subway Company.

Telephone lines: Equipment is maintained by the New York Telephone Company.

Miscellaneous

Map the location of such permanent installations as mailboxes. police and fire alarm boxes, manholes, standpipes, hydrants, lamp posts, oil and coal delivery openings and such semi-permanent or movable items as litter baskets and other trash receptacles, sign posts, kiosks benches and other street furniture.

Outside, professional researchers are available—for a fee—to provide you with maps showing the location of surface and subsurface utility lines and equipment. Professionals can also, of course, do the other research, but you are better off with volunteers from the block.

To make a survey of such factors as street use and maintenance, your observers should station themselves in mid-block, preferably on the second or third floor of a building so they can see both sidewalks and the street from one end of the block to the other.

When each observer has completed his observations from this vantage point, he should walk the entire length of the block slowly, up and down both sides of the street, checking his findings from this close-up point of view. When applicable, he should question passers-by about those aspects of the survey to which he has been assigned.

The survey should be made for a 12-hour period, from 8 a.m. to 8 p.m., on a weekday and again on a weekend day, in each of the four seasons, if possible (the initial survey is really only a beginning; additional ones are needed to keep track of progress and to monitor the feelings of your neighbors).

Once the questionnaires have been returned and the information organized you can begin to make plans. Try to arrange to have meetings at least once a month, and to publicize them extensively, to keep as many people as possible informed—and to get them involved. The more people participate, the greater will be the base of support for the plans as they emerge.

At the monthly meetings encourage people to come up with ideas, offer suggestions or criticism, sketch out priorities, make timetables. Invite members of your Community Planning Board to attend, and extend invitations to property owners, including—perhaps even especially—those who don't live on the block. You don't want anyone saying later "I never knew about those plans."

If you plan outdoor meetings make sure you set a rain date (or have an indoor alternative available).

And the plans themselves? That's next.

5 • What are the options?

Though revitalizing or enlivening a block can involve tearing down buildings or creating fully landscaped parks, such projects are far beyond the scope of a block association. If experience—especially successful experience—is a reliable guide, we must conclude that there are, basically, six ways in which a block association can make a neighborhood more livable.

1	Through temporary street closings.
2	By decorating and redecorating—using fabric, paint and other materials.
3	By placing attractive and useful furnishings—such as baskets, benches and play equipment—in the right places.
4	By using flowers, plants, and trees.
5	By lighting and paving.
6	By converting abandoned lots and other empty spaces into parks or play areas.

Each of these methods can involve problems, and it is better to be aware of those problems at the start than to find out about them when you are already well into your project; you may be forced to back off, or even find yourself in financial or legal difficulty. Take note, then, of the advice that goes along with the ideas suggested.

Temporary street closings

Your street can be closed to traffic, or to traffic and parking, for special events such as block parties, street fairs and clean-up drives, or for special status, such as play street or PAL play street.

Fairs, festivals and other one-day events

Usually, festivals and block parties mean closing a street to traffic and parking for one day between 2 p.m. and 10 p.m. The range of activities possible is virtually without limit, especially if you have active participation by a good percentage of the block's residents (you will find that even those who don't live on your block are eager to lend a hand—block parties seem to bring out the best in people). Schools, community groups, commercial groups and religious organizations frequently are willing to donate time, talent and even money to help you make your block event a success.

In addition to food—which seems to be the first thing that pops to mind when anyone mentions street festivals—there can be other attractions. Consider, just for starters, the following:

Contests

chalk-drawing on the streets	music
costumes	quiz shows
make-up	

Exhibits

films and slides	prints and print-making
paintings	sculpture
photographs	

Demonstrations

Chinese pottery	kite-making (and flying)
clay work	macrame
gardening	silk-screening
glass-blowing	spinning
karate	weaving

Entertainment (almost everything falls within the category of entertainment —if it is entertaining—but some activities, such as macrame or chalk-drawing, involve instruction or competition as well; the suggestions that follow are more in the realm of pure fun)

acrobats	Punch and Judy or other
folk and ethnic music and dance	marionette shows
children's ballets	rock groups
fashion shows	steel bands
palm-reading and other	story-telling
fortune-telling	wandering minstrels

759•7770 DEPARTMENT OF COMMERCE & INDUSTRY

 433•3863 DEPARTMENT OF SOCIAL SERVICES

Information tables can be set up (you are sure to find among your neighbors people who are more than eager to tell others what they know about—well, you name it: ecology, education, health, pie-making). Local merchants can be called upon to help with the decorating, perhaps supplying bunting or banners. Friends and neighbors can provide other decorations, such as signs, posters, flags, flowers and papier-mache sculpture.

Now about that advice: block gatherings cannot be held if there is a hospital or firehouse on the street, or if the street is part of a bus route.

To get permission to close a street temporarily, contact the Street Fair Permit Division of the city's Department of Commerce and Industry or the Economic Development Administration.

If you plan to use any sound systems or devices you must get a permit from the Division of Licenses of the Police Department.

And if you want to raise funds during the street fair you need the permission of the Public Solicitation Section of the Department of Social Services.

Play street closings	By turning a street into a play street, you create a safe (traffic and parking are prohibited on play streets) playground for outdoor activities. The variety of activities is limited only by the imagination of the children—and children have all-but-boundless imaginations.

Before you start on your play-street program, however, there are two absolute "musts" that have to be dealt with.

1	Most of the residents—at least one more than 50 percent—must favor the idea of a play street (they must sign a petition later to prove this);
2	Two adults must be willing to supervise the children at play on the block during the play-street closing hours. You will probably need a large pool of people from which to draw, so that at least two will be on duty at all required times.

566●3600 MAYOR'S OFFICE OF NEIGHBORHOOD GOVERNMENT

 677●1400 POLICE ATHLETIC LEAGUE

And even fulfilling those requirements won't help if your street has some of the following, because their presence means play-street closings are prohibited:

active driveways
broken curbs
commercial establishments
garages or parking lots that must be used during play-street hours
high volume of traffic
parking meters
two-way traffic

If your block is free of these prohibiting factors, if you have the consent of most of the residents and if you have your pool of people from which to draw your two adult supervisors, you are ready to go ahead. What next?

Next, if you plan a summer play-street program, you contact—in April, at the latest—a representative of the Play Street program at the Mayor's Office of Neighborhood Government, or of the Police Athletic League of the Police Department.

You must be able to show that your block has a high-density population, that there are no nearby recreational facilities and that there are no funds available to pay for play equipment.

Once you have met all the requirements and obtained all the necessary permissions, you can proceed. A regular play street is open —that is, closed to traffic and parking—from 8 a.m. to 8 p.m. in the summer months (June through September); a PAL play street's hours are 12:30 p.m. to 8 p.m. in the summer months. Eventually, it's hoped, play streets can be made off limits to traffic other than during the summer.

During play hours the children will undoubtedly dream up their own games. The list that follows is to give you an idea of what to

PLAY
STREET
CLOSED
⟵⟶

POLICE
DEPT.

expect—though you might have one of your adult supervisors offer suggestions in the unlikely event that the kids run out of ideas:

baby parade	go-cart race	Monopoly	roly poly
badminton	handball	musical chairs	sack race
basketball	Heads-Up	one-legged race	Scrabble
bowling	hide and seek	Perquackey	shuffleboard
boxing	high jump	pet show	skating
broad jump	hit the penny	ping pong	skelley
charades	horseshoes	pin-the-tail	spelling bee
checkers	hop scotch	pogo stick race	Spill & Spell
chess	iron tag	punchball	stickball
Four Score	jig saw	Quibic Quoits	stoopball
geography	Johnny on the	ringalevio	tag
ghost	pony	relay race	volley ball
giant steps	leap frog	roller hockey	wrestling
	monkey in the		
	middle		

Old tires, cable spools, barrels, wooden boxes, benches and other easily obtained and readily stored equipment and furnishings can be brought out during play-street hours. Then, too, mobile units with educational and entertaining exhibits are available.

These units, operated by the Parks, Recreation and Cultural Affairs Administration, can bring puppet shows, movies, arts and crafts workshops and sports facilities to your neighborhood. They come rolling down the street like a sort of glorified camp wagon, stop, unfold, set up camp—and are in business to provide entertainment, instruction and fun. They are available in June on weekends only and during July and August all week. (Interested? For addresses and phone numbers look under "Mobile Units" in the Who-Where appendix at the back of the book.)

Incidentally, before your play-street program gets under way you can organize a clean-up campaign to prepare for or go along with it. (Frequently, after the play-street season ends, residents of the block take a greater interest in street housekeeping because they have acquired a new sense of pride and found that a cleaner street is a

better, more livable one.) If you pick a date and give three weeks' notice to the Environmental Protection Administration—in writing—a clean-up can be arranged for you. Let the administration know not only the date and site, but also the type of equipment you think you'll need for the clean-up.

Another municipal service available in conjunction with play streets is the hydrant spray cap—a piece of equipment second to none during those hot, humid summer days. The cap with special spray nozzle is obtainable from your local police station, fire station or Model Cities agency. And don't forget it's illegal to use a hydrant without one—illegal and dangerous, because of the lowered water pressure, which can be a hazard if water is needed to fight a fire.

School streets

School streets are closed to traffic during school hours. The designation of a school street must be requested by the principal of the school, through the Department of Highways. If you feel the street on which your local school is situated should be designated a school street (such a designation is reserved for schools that have inadequate play yard facilities), contact the principal and ask him to make application.

Decorating

It doesn't really take too much to make an otherwise drab and uninteresting spot attractive. A dash of color—in the form of paint or a bunch of flowers—is sometimes more than enough to do the trick. An uninviting corner can be turned into a tiny oasis of pleasure and comfort with nothing more elaborate than a bright bench or a gaily decorated trash basket.

And it is that kind of touch that can turn a collection of houses into a community, that can turn people into neighbors. Especially when the touches are supplied by the people—when the men, women and children who live on a block give their time and their talent to the job

964●1800 DEPARTMENT OF SANITATION

566●3680 DEPARTMENT OF HIGHWAYS

of making all their lives more enjoyable. When people take paint brushes, hammers, brooms and buckets in hand to improve their neighborhood they do more than clean and decorate their surroundings; they revitalize their own lives, individually and together.

In a very real sense, when you recruit people to work on a block project you are doing them a favor. The man or woman who uses the street only as a route to and from home and office, and who agrees to help hang banners or paint benches or clean up a lot—that person will find a change in outlook. He or she will find a new and active interest in the block, in the neighbors. That man or woman will become part of a community.

Don't be timid about asking for help. When you get it, you are giving it in return.

A banner idea

One way to make your block reflect the way you and your neighbors think is to hang banners between the windows of buildings. Banners add more than color and liveliness; they add a sense of identity.

To hang banners on a building, between windows or in some other flat way, you must, of course, have the permission of the building owner. Then, too, you must check with the Department of Buildings to make sure this is permitted in your area. Naturally, you'll need the cooperation of the people from whose windows your banners are to be hung (and make certain, please, that they don't obstruct fire escapes).

If you want to hang your banners from flag staffs, or span the street with one or more banners, your requests are coordinated through the Department of Commerce and Industry, with final permission coming from the Department of Highways (you will still, of course, need the permission of building owners).

Before you can hang a banner across the street, 50 percent of the block's residents must give their approval. And the banner may not represent a profit-making organization. Cross-street-banner-hanging is one of the few projects in which volunteers may not be used, unless you happen to have a volunteer who is also a professional rigger—because a professional rigger must be used for this kind of work. In addition, a permit must be obtained from the Department of Buildings (this will cost about $30).

759•7770 DEPARTMENT OF COMMERCE & INDUSTRY

Material for banners? Canvas is probably the best bet. Reasonably priced, durable, easy to work with, it comes in a variety of weights and colors. Working out the shape of the banner and the design can be a stimulating community project that is sure to attract and involve many residents of the block.

Painting walls

Few aspects of city life can be more grindingly dull—and few can do more to make monotony seem an inescapable part of the city scene —than the long lines of gray building facades. Their sameness, broken only by street intersections, seems to reflect, or perhaps be part of, the sameness of life.

But life in the city is not dull and monotonous, and there is no reason for buildings to have a dull and monotonous sameness. And you and your block association can do much to ease that monotony, to infuse life and color into the appearance of the buildings in which you and your neighbors live.

Jason Crum, a professional artist who helped create a neighborhood mural, said:

The wall becomes a part of the community. It changes with the light, the weather, the seasons. And the community is part of the painting. Its importance is that after the performance of the actual painting, it remains to reflect the care and thought of the artist and the care and thought of the community, which continues to experience it.

A professional artist who is willing to help is, of course, a great boon. But amateur artists, and even people who have never before tried to paint, can create lively, colorful and often quite beautiful murals. An artist can perhaps direct the discussion of design, pointing out pitfalls that the untrained can't see, or explain some of the mechanics of painting (such as which kinds of paint adhere best to which kinds of surfaces, and which can best withstand the assaults of rain, snow, sunlight, grime and other hazards of outdoor life).

A professional can also train the semi-skilled or unskilled in the use of paints, brushes and other material. Or he can oversee the operation, perhaps creating the design on paper and supervising the execution of the mural.

But even with no professional at hand to explain, train, direct or supervise—with nothing more than willing hands and eager minds—

541●8423 CITY WALLS, INC.

you can turn gray into gay. And in doing so, you may get a bonus in the form of the disappearance of graffiti, a bonus that can be a welcome one indeed.

Your mural can be at street level. It can be a roof-to-ground work, or a design between windows. You are limited only by your imagination—plus the requirements of scaffolding if you plan to go beyond ladder-and-reach height. Scaffolding means professional installations and the use of trained mural painters working on rigs. The entire operation must be properly insured. All of which, naturally, costs money.

But if you confine your mural to a height of, say 15 feet, you can probably get it done entirely with volunteer work, and with none of the hassles of permits, insurance and so on.

With murals, as with other projects, a few precautions and other preliminaries are needed. For example:

● You must get permission from the landlord of the building whose wall you intend to paint.

● If the building is city-owned, you'll need the approval of the City Art Commission, and you'll have to get it through whatever city agency has jurisdiction of the building.

● Make sure you don't use lead-based paints, which are poisonous.

It goes without saying that before any design is executed it will have been discussed, dissected, revised and, finally, approved by those who will be living with it every day—the residents of the block. They must feel that the design, in conception and execution, is a true expression of the community.

You might, incidentally, see what you can get local merchants to contribute toward the project (a general bit of advice that applies not only to murals, but also to any other undertakings that require money or materials or both). At the unveiling—and you should have some kind of ceremony to mark the successful completion—you can perhaps express the block's appreciation. A little goodwill goes a long way.

Finally (a misleading word because, though this is the last paragraph about murals, it should perhaps be the first thing you do), you ought to consult City Walls, Inc. This public-service, tax-exempt

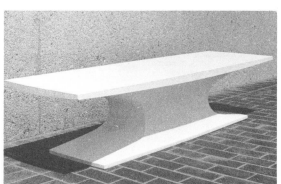

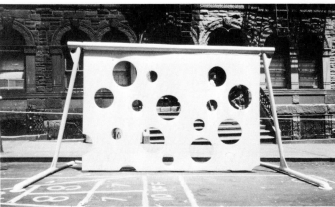

organization will advise you, guide you and even provide or find contractors and artists. Its address, like those of other helpful organizations and agencies, is listed in the back of the book.

Painting
elsewhere

Walls, of course, are marvelously enticing things for would-be painters, with their big stretches of space on which to apply color. But they are not by any means the only things to which to turn with your paint brush or spray can or roller.

Look around. Is there an unused billboard? Paint it (but you must, of course, find out who owns or rents the billboard and get permission). Are there drab or peeling or unpainted planters? Paint them (with permission). GI's at basic training used to say "If it moves, salute it; if it doesn't, paint it." To a certain extent, the last part of that sentence applies to city blocks. If it's paintable, paint it—but always with permission and always with the consent of your neighbors.

Furniture and furnishings

In addition to painting, cleaning and sprucing up what's already there, you can make your block more lively and more livable by adding to its furnishings. It doesn't all have to be done at once—something you'd not be likely to do anyhow—and the gradual addition of bright and useful items can be a continuing process that brings a touch of expectancy and excitement to all. A bench or two one month, perhaps some new and colorful trash receptacles the next. Then planters, play equipment, flowers, trees.

Bit by bit your block can take on a new—and ever-changing—look. It can become, not a route or pass-through, not just another faceless street in a heartless city, but a warm and inviting community.

In addition to the usual advice about getting the permission of building and lot owners and making certain that your neighbors—or most of them—approve, there is some special advice that applies to the use of street furnishings.

For any permanently installed furnishings for streets or on city-owned lots or other property, you must get the approval of the City Art Commission through the city agency having jurisdiction over the property (for streets, as an example, you'd apply for approval through the Department of Highways). In addition, permission must be obtained from the Department of Highways for sidewalk installations.

Any permanently installed furnishings should be covered by liability insurance for personal-property or personal-bodily damage.

Liability insurance may be difficult to get for an individual block. But if you buy your furnishings and equipment through the Parks Council (listed in the Who-Where section of the appendix) you can participate in the Council's blanket-coverage policy.

The Parks Council is a non-profit, tax-exempt organization whose goal is making the city a better place in which to live. Contributions to it are legitimate tax deductions. Instead of buying furnishings or equipment on the commercial market, you can buy it through the Council, and the money given to the Council is a tax deduction—a point that should be stressed when you are soliciting for funds.

To keep your insurance valid and in force, you must:

1	Keep the furnishings in a safe place.
2	Maintain them properly so they don't become hazardous to use.
3	Make sure, if children's play equipment is involved, that a competent adult is present at all times to supervise the children.

Equipment that is not permanently installed should be stored when not being used, and you must arrange for storage space. You'll also need a pool of volunteers to help maintain the furnishings and tend the flowers and trees. Storage should be no problem; seasonal equipment can be stored out of season in church cellars, store fronts, garages and in people's closets.

Sidewalk furnishings must not, of course, jut out into the street or otherwise become potential impediments to the free movement of vehicles, and they must not block access to surface and sub-surface facilities, including the following:

surface
alarm boxes
fire hydrants
fuel delivery openings
manholes
rubbish and garbage deposit areas
siamese connections (two-pipe
    connection outlets leading from
    a single water pipe)

sub-surface
gas mains
lighting conduits
power transmission lines
sanitary sewers
steam pipes
storm sewers
telegraph duct lines
telephone cables
water mains

The furnishings must not impede normal pedestrian flow or require major pedestrian detours. They must not distract drivers or obstruct their view. And, finally, they must not be dangerous to use and must be durable enough to withstand heavy use and the onslaughts of weather.

With all these precautions taken, and once you have the go-ahead from your neighbors, you are ready to furnish your block.

Trash receptacles

To start your furnishings, why not consider trash receptacles? Not only can bright and decorative trash receptacles improve, by themselves, the appearance of your block, but they will also help to overcome the litter problem. They do, in effect, double duty.

Attractive, modern, lined receptacles are already showing up in parts of the city, as replacements for, or additions, to, old litter baskets. Under a new program sponsored by the Environmental Protection Administration, organizations and individuals can donate litter baskets bearing the donor's name (the donor must take responsibility for the care and maintenance of the basket).

If private carters, or volunteers, empty your receptacles you have virtually no restrictions on size, shape or material (though you are obviously bound by the rules of reason and function). But if the city Sanitation Department is to do the servicing, your receptacles must meet certain minimum standards. Here they are:

- The receptacle cannot be permanently installed (attached, for example, to a light pole, or screwed into the ground, or even weighted down with bricks).
- It must not weigh more than 50 pounds or less than 15 pounds and its capacity must not exceed 5 cubic feet.
- For receptacles designed to have an inner liner, neither the outer nor inner part may weigh more than 50 pounds.
- No receptacle may require the use of a lock or key device to be emptied.
- No receptacle may require the use of paper or plastic bags.
- Provision must be made for drainage of the receptacle.

You can buy trash receptacles that meet these standards through the Parks Council. While you're supplying your block with new trash containers—and even before—you might start a clean-street campaign. Encourage your neighbors to use paper or plastic refuse bags for their household throw-outs. The ones that meet city specifications carry a "clean" symbol. Using these bags will help not only to keep the street clean, but to keep it more quiet, as well (and it helps to make sanitation collections cleaner, quicker and more efficient).

Here are some other suggestions for a cleaner street:

- If trash pick-ups aren't regular, contact the Department of Sanitation.

- If street drains are clogged, contact the Department of Water Resources.

- If sidewalks are in disrepair, urge the owners to have them fixed. Owners are required by law to keep the sidewalks that abut their buildings in good repair. If the owners balk or put you off or fail to deliver on promises, complain to the Department of Highways.

- If the street has potholes, tell it to the Department of Highways.

- If there's a littered alley or an abandoned car on the block, call the Department of Sanitation to have the alley cleaned up or the car hauled away. As for vacant lots—littered or otherwise—do nothing until you've read the section, later in this chapter, on what to do with these potentially valuable unnatural resources.

Seating

Another useful piece of street furniture—and one that will be highly appreciated—is a bench or other kind of seat. It doesn't take a trained observer to see that people use whatever comes to hand— packing cases, stoops, boxes, piles of bricks—to plunk themselves down on for a bit of relaxation, or to rest feet weary from shopping. Give these people a safe, comfortable, cheerful and inviting place to sit and you will have spread a bit of that feeling of human togetherness that, at its best, can make a city a home.

Be sure to place seating where it will not be exposed to blasts of wind or—unless you have sunbathers in mind—the direct rays of the sun (and here is one place where your block survey will provide the needed information). For the installation of permanent chairs or benches, the kind that are bolted or weighted down, you'll need the approval of the City Art Commission and the permission of the Department of Highways.

Like trash receptacles, benches and other seating can be bought —again with tax advantages—through the Parks Council.

Play equipment

When it comes to play and playground equipment you must be prepared to lay out money, either for purchasing the equipment or for installing it, or both. Of course there is play equipment that costs little, or even nothing, but you will have to invest in time, effort and ingenuity. Some of the cost-free items that come to mind are discarded tires (which make wonderful swings and crawl-through things) and packing cases (which make marvelous castles, climb-on things and other play items). The packing cases must be carefully inspected for nails, splinters and other hazards, and must be just as carefully reinforced and refinished. Then, of course, there are those old standbys, rope, sand, soil and water.

Play equipment without moveable parts is generally safer, as is see-through equipment (which reduces the chances of someone's being surprised by a child darting out from behind it, and the chances of an adult's using the equipment as a hiding place).

The Parks Council, once more, can provide the equipment while offering a tax saving.

If your street can't accommodate playground equipment because it is too narrow, too crowded or ineligible for play-street status, there is still the possibility of using vacant space. And for more about vacant lots, turn to page 61.

Plants and trees

There is nothing quite like living color to brighten your block—the color of living flowers and trees. Somehow, a growing, breathing thing can generate feelings that no manmade furnishings can. Perhaps it's the feeling of kinship that exists between fellow creatures, fellow passengers on the spaceship Earth. Perhaps it's the awe and wonder at the miracle of life, the knowledge that man—despite his cleverness and sophistication—can never duplicate in all its subtlety and beauty even the simplest of nature's creations.

Whatever the reasons, plants can do wonders to make your block more beautiful and life on it more congenial.

You can start the greening of your block with simple planters and inexpensive flowers. Ask your neighbors what they'd like to see, and whether they'd be willing to put flower pots or planters in their windows. Ask building owners for permission to put planters on their

property. Perhaps you can get together with your neighbors—a meeting of the block association is a good occasion—to coordinate your colors.

You may have an expert—amateur or professional—among you who would be able to advise everyone about which plants would be likely to do best, which require what kinds of care and how they would look in the different stages of their growth. With or without such home-grown help you can turn for assistance to the Department of Parks, the Parks Council and to the information services of the Botanic Gardens.

Permission for the installation of sidewalk and other planters must be obtained from property owners (whether private or municipal) and from the Departments of Parks and Highways.

Trees are really worth a book all by themselves. Perhaps several books; one about how much they can do for your block, another about the benefits they provide that aren't even considered (like fresher air and the songs of birds), still another about caring for them. But obviously our remarks will be confined to a few brief paragraphs, and the first of these will be on the kind of tree to select.

The Parks Department recommends any of these 12 kinds:

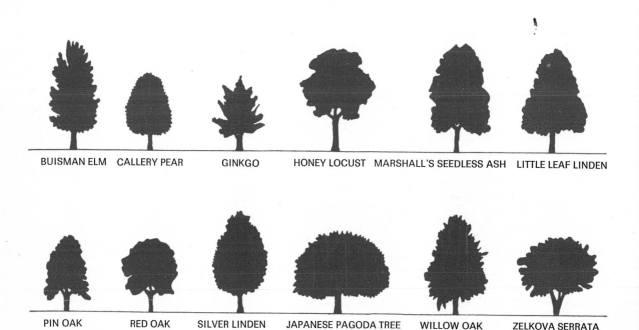

BUISMAN ELM   CALLERY PEAR   GINKGO   HONEY LOCUST   MARSHALL'S SEEDLESS ASH   LITTLE LEAF LINDEN

PIN OAK   RED OAK   SILVER LINDEN   JAPANESE PAGODA TREE   WILLOW OAK   ZELKOVA SERRATA

799●6000 PARKS COUNCIL

There are acceptable substitutes, and the Parks Department will advise you about them and recommend the kind best suited to your area.

If the tree you want to plant is on the list, you must obtain a permit from the Department of Highways. If it is not, on the list, you must apply for your permit in writing—not by telephone—to the Department of Parks in your borough. The department's horticulturist will make a survey for you, give you a planting permit, suggest several possible tree contractors and, once the tree has been planted, inspect it for you.

Whatever tree you select, if you plan to plant it along the block—you could, of course, plant it on private property—it must be at least 2½ inches in diameter at a point six inches above the ground. The sidewalk at that point ought to be at least eight feet wide so that pedestrians will not be crowded by the tree.

Don't forget that trees grow and that they need air, water and light. Make sure you leave space at the base—an open area or an open-work grill—for water to get down to the roots. You should protect the base with bricks tilted in towards the tree and kept at the same grade as the sidewalk (so no one will trip over them), fencing and warning signs to discourage dog-walkers.

Some of the problems (such as dogs) can be circumvented by using planters instead of sticking your tree directly into the ground. Once more, you need permission from the owner of the property in front of which you want to place your planter, plus that of the Departments of Parks and Highways. (If you install the planters through the Parks Council the Parks Department permit is not necessary. Insurance on planters—which is required—can be obtained through the Council too. And, of course, the trees themselves can be bought, with all the accompanying tax advantages, through the Council.)

Hoops, ground-covering and continuing maintenance can also be arranged on a tax-deductible basis through the Council.

If your tree-planting and other beautification programs total $5,000 or more, your tax-deductible contributions can be made through the Salute to the Seasons Fund for a More Beautiful New York (whose address, of course, is listed in the back).

If you and your neighbors can raise only a limited tree fund, you can still go ahead with your planting by taking advantage of the tree-matching program of the Parks, Recreation and Cultural Affairs Administration. The administration will plant trees on your street if your block association, or a group of residents, can raise $200. (See "Tree Matching Program" in the who-where list at the back.)

Remember—especially if you start to become discouraged—one tree has more impact on the eyes and heart of a New Yorker than a whole grove has on a rural homeowner.

Lights and paving

Another bright idea—literally—for your block is to improve the lighting. You can start with a project that costs nothing: getting the city to correct deficiencies in the lighting equipment that is already on your block. If some of the street lamps aren't working, or don't work properly, write to the director of the Bureau of Gas and Electricity, giving as much detail as you can about existing conditions and how you think they can be upgraded. (The block survey will be a good guide here—it should show what needs to be done.)

Better lighting means not only a brighter and more attractive street, it also discourages crime and encourages people to make fuller use of their block in the evening. And, like the other projects outlined here, it can generate interest in its planning stages, drawing people into an active role in the community and creating a new and exciting sense of involvement.

The Bureau of Gas and Electricity, which is part of the Department of Public Works, does more than listen to and act on complaints about faulty municipal lighting equipment. It can also give you information and guidance about private lighting. Such lighting can be not only functional, it can also be decorative, adding a touch of grace and beauty to your block.

To install floodlights, lanterns or other equipment on private property, you will, naturally, need the permission of the property owner. The work must be done by a licensed electrician and the lights must be placed so that they do not pose a hazard. And, of course, they must not be installed so as to shine directly into anyone's window.

With bright murals, colorful flowers, inviting trees, new trash receptacles, benches and play equipment and cheerful lights, things ought to be looking up on your block. So how about looking down for a

while—down at the pavement. It doesn't have to have that city sameness, any more than other aspects of your block.

New paving can be the frosting on the cake, the finishing touch to your physical revitalization of the block.

What's available? Brick (in a variety of textures and colors), cobblestone and limestone, patio block, cube-shaped granite, colored asphalt, flagstone, concrete paving blocks, pre-cast concrete slabs.

You can brighten up driveways, alleys, sections of sidewalk, pave over parts of vacant lots. The City Arts Workshop (listed, of course, in the back) can give you advice and assistance.

Though you probably won't have the space for such a project, consider, if for nothing more than inspiration, the "Patchwork Plaza" in Washington Square Park. Users of the park were invited to arrange, in patterns of their choice, vividly colored venetian-glass chips, or to etch their own designs in triangular modules. The end product was a plaza 40 feet in diameter made of 700 two-foot equilateral triangles.

This is the kind of project in which an entire community can become excitingly involved. It doesn't have to be big; just a couple of square feet of sidewalk is all that's needed. That, plus the right spirit.

Using vacant lots

There are few sites more full of potential for revitalization than a vacant lot. There it stands—empty, except for litter, an eyesore, dangerous perhaps (broken glass and tin-can tops can be lethal)—ready to be converted into a garden, a minipark, a playground, a ballfield, even an outdoor theater.

Perhaps, too, the sidewalks on your block are too narrow to accommodate some of the furnishings you and your neighbors would like to provide. The vacant lot is your answer. Un-vacant it!

All you need is time, willingness, not too much money, a little ingenuity, helping hands. And permission.

Permission, because there is really no such animal as an ownerless lot. Vacant, yes; abandoned, yes. But ownerless? No. Someone, somewhere, owns every piece of real estate. If not a private party, then a government agency or a corporation.

To install permanent fixtures, such as playground equipment, lights and so on, in a city-owned lot you must get the approval of the City Art Commission through the city agency that has jurisdiction over the site. If you are uncertain about who has jurisdiction, contact the Mayor's Office of Neighborhood Government. That same office will provide, through its Playlots Project, free assistance and equipment for grading, fencing, paving and installing playground equipment. The Playlots Project encourages community groups to work up their own playground designs, and it offers maintenance and repair service for lots developed through its program.

Another useful source of help and guidance is the Parks Council, which, for one dollar, will send you its vacant-lot guidebook, ''A Little About Lots.'' This booklet outlines the important steps involved in converting lots into pleasant, useful, beautiful places.

Turning a dangerous, ugly and unsanitary eyesore into a source of neighborhood pride, pleasure and fun is not an idle dream. It has been done many times in many neighborhoods by many people. It can be done by you.

6 • Maintaining the momentum

Once you and your neighbors have agreed on the kind of project you want, you must see it through to completion. Progress reports, of course, should be made at least monthly, either at block-association meetings or at other kinds of gatherings at which a good representation of residents and owners can attend. The prime rule is: Keep as many people as you can as informed as you can. Listen to suggestions and ideas and try to remain flexible, incorporating into your plans any workable new ideas that seem to have general appeal and approval.

Keep a record of your progress. One way to do this is to use a "flow chart," copies of which can be distributed at meetings to keep everyone up to date. Your flow chart should show the tasks that have been assigned, the people to whom they have been assigned, the starting date, the proposed completion date, work accomplished thus far, permits or licenses needed for work that remains and, if necessary, other comments.

If your plans require a designer, architect, electrician or other professional, advertise in local papers, with notices in supermarkets and by word of mouth to get as much volunteer help as possible. Sometimes, of course, your efforts will get you nowhere (perhaps because there is no qualified professional living in your area) and you then must turn to paid help. Architectural assistance can sometimes be had from schools of architecture, whose students are eager for experience and willing to work for virtually nothing to get it. The Architects' Technical Assistance Center (see the appendix for address and phone number) also provides advice and assistance.

You should do a complete breakdown of costs, including in your estimate not only the cost of furnishings and other equipment, but also such factors as clerical help, installation, insurance, paint and other construction materials, permits, office supplies, publicity, repairs and replacement and—easily overlooked but of great importance—maintenance.

In figuring your costs on permanent installations, such as the placing of heavy playground equipment, you would be wise to add one-third to one-half the purchase price to allow for installation fees and materials. It may seem high, but it's better to err on the high side than to find yourself out of funds at some crucial stage.

With a good idea of costs to work with, study fund-raising sources both on and off the block to see how well your revenues are likely to match your expenses. (For fund-raising ideas consult the next chapter.)

Determine which city agencies must be consulted, for advice, assistance and, of course, permits and approvals. Give these agencies, in writing, all the necessary details, including:

1	Evidence of large-scale support on your block.
2	Evidence of need for block improvement.
3	Results of your street studies, if pertinent.
4	Evidence of money in hand or of the likelihood of its being in hand.
5	A reasonably detailed summary of your goals and of the timetable you have set for reaching those goals.

Keep in touch with those agencies as you go forward, so they can advise and guide you and let you know well in advance what parts of your plans might run into legal, bureaucratic or physical trouble and how to avoid or minimize the trouble. Don't overlook the possibility of getting help from the offices of elected officials, such as your Councilman, Assemblyman, State Senator or Borough President.

7 • Finding the funds

Although many projects can be done at virtually no cost, you will still need to raise funds. The no-cost projects and the minimal-cost projects, especially if they are successful, will lure you to bigger, more elaborate planning and, eventually, you'll need money. This chapter is meant to help you find it.

But before we go into the how's of raising money, suppose we take a brief look at what money can do. What, for example, could you do with, say, $500? You could do any one of the following:

- Plant 10 trees, put in two benches and add some vines and a small garden to your block.

- Get a giant vacuum cleaner to keep your street neater, and install a bicycle rack or a community bulletin board.

- Paint a small mural and add new lighting on a modest scale.

- Put in three or four planters, with flowers or small shrubs.

- Plant about 150 flowers or plants in building-front gardens.

- Begin a community garden if you have a vacant lot, or place the first few small pieces of children's play equipment.

The ideas are just a small—a very small—sample. Your neighbors will undoubtedly be able to suggest other ways of using money, and by bouncing ideas around, and learning through shopping and other experience, you will be able to expand the list a hundredfold.

Now on to fund-raising.

To begin with, here is an idea of sources to which to turn for money:

- residents of the block
- local churches and synagogues
- local merchants (you need not confine your search to your block; merchants and businessmen in nearby areas can also be approached; your Chamber of Commerce can supply you with a listing)
- local planning board
- neighborhood and community umbrella organizations, such as civic groups, environmental organizations, etc.
- contacts outside the neighborhood

And to continue, here is only a sampling of the kinds of events you can sponsor or organize for fund-raising:

- block parties
- white elephant and tag or garage sales
- talent shows
- trick-or-treating (at the right time of year, naturally)
- carolling (ditto)
- food sales
- rummage sales
- recycling programs (these do double or triple duty; not only can you raise funds, but you help clean up your community and promote better conservation practices)
- outings and excursions

Don't turn up your nose at the dimes and dollars such solicitation and events can raise. They add up, sometimes more quickly than you hope.

In soliciting donations, especially for specific projects or purchases, stress to your potential donors that funds can be contributed through the Parks Council, which appeals not only to the donor's civic sense, but to his pocketbook sense as well, because $10 or $100 (or 10 cents) given to you by way of the Council can be written off as a tax deduction.

For further information about recycling programs and how they can be used to raise funds (aluminum products—cans, trays and so on—bring about 10 cents a pound, glass about a penny a pound) contact the Environmental Action Coalition, whose address is at the back of the book.

Now then—big money. How do you get it?

City, state and federal government agencies, corporations and foundations are your best sources for large amounts of money in big lumps. This can come in the form of "matching grants"—as in the case of the tree-planting program—or it can be an outright donation.

The principal difference between knocking on doors or asking your local merchants, and approaching government agencies or foundations, is that in the latter case you'll need a somewhat slicker (the fashionable phrase is "more professional") approach. You may even have to hire a professional fund-raiser or lawyer who knows his way around the fund-raising world, which is a complicated one in which many an amateur has become lost.

That doesn't mean you can't try it yourself. But it does mean you must go about it carefully, submitting a written proposal, which should —it goes without saying—be neatly typed and include the following information:

- Location of the block.

- Description of the neighborhood.

- Evidence that the project would satisfy a grave need for recreation areas for children, relaxation space for the elderly, open space in crowded conditions, or whatever the residents of your block feel is the most vital need. Thus, you must provide evidence, for example, that there are no parks or playgrounds nearby or that, if there are, they are inaccessible to the residents of your block.

- Description of community participation and evidence of support for the project.

- Statistics on the number of people living on your block, including a breakdown by age range—especially children and the elderly.

- Statistics on the total number of local people you believe will benefit from the project.

- Description of the street—its dimensions and the number and type of buildings.

- Description of the studies you have made of the street, its residents, its needs, its physical aspects.

- Description of the environmental and social significance of the plan—the positive influences you believe it will have on the block.

- Details—as many as you can supply—of the long-range plans you have for the block.

- A copy of the potential design for the final street scene.

- A photograph of the street as it is now.

- A complete breakdown of costs for your plan, including costs of insurance, maintenance and repairs likely to be necessitated by vandalism. Include figures on how much you have raised and are likely to raise through local efforts.

Bear in mind that the Parks Council, which exists for the express purpose of encouraging and helping New Yorkers to improve the urban environment, is willing to tackle any job costing any amount. It will save you money by pre-clearing your projects with the appropriate city agencies, supervising all aspects of permit applications, ordering, installing and maintaining equipment, providing insurance at the lowest possible cost and giving you professional, well-thought-out advice on all your projects, large or small.

The Salute to the Seasons Fund for a More Beautiful New York is available for assistance on major projects—those costing over $5,000. And remember, too, to remind potential donors that they can give to you through the Council or the Salute to the Seasons Fund.

Appendices

The questionnaire

Here is a sample of the kind
of questionnaire that will
help you take the pulse of
your block.

Dear Neighbor:

Some of your neighbors on the block are interested in improving it by
making it more attractive. Your answers to the following questions are to
let us know if you are interested in the idea as well, what you feel should
be done, and how much you'd be willing to do to improve it. We'll get
back to you with the results of the questionnaire shortly.

   Thank you!

   Please return the completed questionnaire to either (give the name and
address of the president of the block association or the temporary leader
if one hasn't been elected yet) or (give the name and address of the vice
president of the association or another temporary officer or leader).

   1. How long have you lived on the block?_____
   2. Do you like living on the block?_____
   3. Do you rent or own the place where you live?_____
   4. Do you work?_____   If so, what do you do?_____
      _____
   5. Age_____   Male or female_____
   6. How many people live with you?_____
   7. What are their ages and sexes? _____
   8. Do you find the block attractive-looking?_____ unattractive?_____
      neither? _____

9. Do you ever use the street as a place to chat, sit in the sun, play games? Please describe briefly the ways in which you use your street.

    _____

    _____

10. If additions were made on the street, which of the following would you like to see:

    a) additional lighting ____   e) more attractive paving ____

    b) banners ____   f) painted wall murals ____

    c) benches or seats ____   g) fresh paint on fences,

    d) community bulletin board ____   building fronts, etc. ____

    h) trees and plants ____

11. If a vacant lot on the block or nearby is available, would you like to see it cleaned up, decorated and turned into

    a) a small park ____   c) a garden ____

    b) a playground ____

12. If street changes are made, should they be designed especially to serve any of these groups: children ____ elderly people ____ young adults ____ adults ____ teenagers ____ everyone ____

13. Where on the block would you like to see changes? At the ends (which one? or both?) ____ in the middle ____ elsewhere ____ (please say where) _____

14. Do you think the kinds of changes suggested in this questionnaire would be popular or unpopular on the block? _____
    Please give the reasons for your answer: _____

    _____

    _____

    _____

15. Would you help to make the street more attractive by contributing time? ____ money? _____

16. Do you have a skill that would be useful in making changes on the block, such as carpentry, masonry, painting, sewing, designing, working with electricity? _____

17. Would you be willing to volunteer this skill—using your own talents and perhaps teaching or supervising others—to help improve the block?_____

18. Are you in a profession whose services might be of use to a block association (such as law, insurance, communications)?_____

19. Would you be willing to contribute time and advice to help your block association in a professional capacity?_____

20. Do you have any suggestions for improving the block?_____

_____

_____

_____

_____

_____

_____

_____

_____

_____

_____

_____

_____

Please fill in and
return this questionnaire
at your earliest
convenience.

And, again, thank you.

Who-where

Abandoned car removal

Cars with license plates: local police station.
Cars without license plates: Dep't. of Sanitation, 964-1800.

Air pollution

See Environmental Protection Administration.

Architects' Technical Assistance Center, Inc.

20 West 40th St., N.Y., N.Y. 10018, 594-0259 (provides design and architectural advice and help to community organizations that cannot afford such professional services; see also Architecture and design, schools of).

Architecture and design, schools of

High School of Art and Design, 1075 2d Ave., N.Y., N.Y. 10022, 752-4340.

Pratt Institute of Design, 215 Ryerson Ave., Bklyn., N.Y. 11205, 622-2200.

School of Architecture, City College, 133d St. & Bwy., N.Y., N.Y. 10027, 621-2118-9.

School of Architecture, Columbia Univ., 405 Avery Hall, N.Y., N.Y. 10028, 280-3504.

School of Architecture, Cooper Union, 4th Ave. & 7th St., N.Y., N.Y. 10003, 254-6300.

Art Commission, City

Commission approval, needed for permanent furnishings or art work on city-owned buildings or property, is ob-

tainable through the city agency having jurisdiction over the property. See individual agencies.

Art works on the street, advice on

Public Arts Council, 25 Central Park West, N.Y., N.Y. 10023, 541-8423.

Automobiles, abandoned

See Abandoned car removal.

Banners

On buildings: apply in person (not by phone or mail) at Dep't. of Buildings at

BRONX: 1932 Arthur Ave.
BROOKLYN: Municipal Building.
MANHATTAN: Municipal Building, room 2022.
QUEENS: 126-06 Queens Blvd., Kew Gardens.
RICHMOND: Borough Hall.

Across streets: apply to Dep't. of Highways, Permit Clerk's Office, at

BRONX: CY 3-9000.
BROOKLYN: 643-7806.
MANHATTAN: 566-2006-7.
QUEENS: 258-5000.
RICHMOND: 390-5152.

Barbecues on the street

Must not be within 10 feet of any combustible material. Garden hose attached to water supply, or 16-quart pail of water, must be kept at hand. If in doubt, ask at local firehouse.

Block associations

For advice on forming and running an association, see Neighborhood Government, Mayor's Office of.

Bocci

For permit to build a bocci court: Dep't. of Consumer Affairs, 80 Lafayette St., N.Y., N.Y. 10007, 566-5360.

Botanic gardens

BRONX: Bronx Park, Bronx, N.Y. 10458, 933-9400.
BROOKLYN: 1000 Washington Ave., Bklyn., N.Y. 11225, 622-4433.
QUEENS: 43-50 Main St., Flushing, N.Y. 11355, 886-3800.

Buildings, Dep't of

BRONX: 1932 Arthur Ave., Bronx, N.Y. 10457, 583-5520.
BROOKLYN: Municipal Bldg., 8th floor, Brooklyn, N.Y. 11020, 643-7944.
MANHATTAN: Municipal Bldg., 20th floor, N.Y., N.Y. 10007, 566-2384.
QUEENS: 126-06 Queens Blvd., Kew Gardens, N.Y. 11415, 268-5000.
RICHMOND: Borough Hall, Staten Island, N.Y. 10301, 390-5179.

Buildings, ownership

To identify owners of buildings: go in person to City Register office at

BRONX: 851 Grand Concourse.
BROOKLYN: Municipal Building.
MANHATTAN: 31 Chambers St.
QUEENS: 161-04 Jamaica Ave., Jamaica.
RICHMOND: Borough Hall.

Canopies over sidewalks

Dep't. of Highways. (See Highways, Dep't. of, for borough offices).

Cars, abandoned

See Abandoned car removal.

Catch-basin backups

Dep't. of Water Resources.

Chamber of Commerce

For address of your local Chamber, call 732-1123.

Cityarts Workshop, Inc.

830 5th Ave., N.Y., N.Y. 10021, 360-8214 (for information on "Patchwork Plaza" paving).

City Walls, Inc.

25 Central Park West, N.Y., N.Y. 10023, 541-8423 (for advice and help in painting murals on buildings).

Cleanups

Bulk pickups: Dep't. of Sanitation, 964-1800.

For special block cleanup days, write to Block Cleanup Request, Environmental Protection Administration, 2352 Municipal Building, N.Y., N.Y. 10007. Provide date or dates (allow three weeks' notice), time, place and kind of equipment desired.

Vacant lots: see Lots, vacant.

Commerce and Industry, Dep't. of

415 Madison Ave., N.Y., N.Y. 10017, 759-7770.

Community Makers

13 West 89th St., N.Y., N.Y. 10024 (send $1.00 for copy of "Your Block Is a Play Street").

Community Planning Boards

To find your local board, call your Borough President's office at

BRONX: 293-9000.
BROOKLYN: 643-2054.
MANHATTAN: 566-4300.
QUEENS: 268-5000.
RICHMOND: 390-5100.

Council on the Environment of New York City

51 Chambers St., N.Y., N.Y. 10007, 566-0990.

Curbs, broken

Send written complaints to Dep't. of Highways, 40 Worth St., N.Y., N.Y. 10013, Room 818. Enclose stamped, self-addressed envelope.

Entertainment

For information on free events in your neighborhood call Parks, Recreation and Cultural Affairs Administration, 472-1003.

For requests for mobile units (during summer months), offering puppet shows, films, sports and arts and crafts, call or go to the Dep't. of Recreation at

BRONX: Administration Building, Bronx Park East and Birchall Ave., Bronx, N.Y. 10462, TA 8-3200.

BROOKLYN: Litchfield Mansion, Prospect Park West and 5th St., Bklyn., N.Y. 11215, SO 8-2300.

MANHATTAN: 280 Broadway, N.Y., N.Y. 10007, DI 9-6890, or The Arsenal, 830 5th Ave., 360-8215.

QUEENS: The Overlook, Union Tpke. and Park Lane, Kew Gardens, N.Y. 11415, LI 4-4400.

RICHMOND: 1150 Clove Rd., Staten Island, N.Y. 10301, 442-7640.

For mobile stages with lighting, call 360-8196.

For information on mobile units or stages from September through May, call Dep't. of Recreation Mobile Recreation Program, 830 5th Ave., 360-8215 or 360-8218.

For N.Y. Public Library bookmobile, available year-round, inquire at 10 Hyatt St., Staten Island, N.Y. 10301, 442-8562, or 2555 Marion Ave., N.Y., N.Y. 10458.

For American Museum of Natural History educational van, write to the chairman, Dep't. of Education, American Museum of Natural History, Central Park West and 79th St., N.Y., N.Y. 10024, or call 873-1300 extension 341.

Environmental Action Coalition

For information on environmental matters and copies of "Environmental Survival Kit" and information about "Trash Is Cash" program, 235 East 49th St., N.Y., N.Y. 10017, 486-9550.

Environmental complaints

See Environmental Protection Administration

Environmental Protection Administration

Cleanups, 566-5244 (after 1 p.m.).

Complaints about water or air quality, sewers or noise pollution, 966-7500.

General offices, 2358 Municipal Building, N.Y., N.Y. 10007, 566-4124.

Extermination

For complaints about rodents, insects or weeds, Bureau of Pest Control, Dep't. of Health, 566-7726-7-8-9.

Fairs and Festivals

For permit: apply to Dep't. of Commerce and Industry, 415 Madison Ave., N.Y., N.Y. 10017, 759-7770.

For permits to raise funds at street fairs: apply to Dep't. of Social Services, 433-3863.

Fire Dep't.

In emergencies, dial 911, or

BRONX: 665-2200.
BROOKLYN: 636-1700.
MANHATTAN: 628-2900.
QUEENS: 847-6600.
RICHMOND: 727-1100.

Flowers and plants

For advice on selection, planting and care, see Botanic Gardens, Horticultural Society of New York and Parks, Recreation and Cultural Affairs Administration.

For permits to install planters, see Parks, Recreation and Cultural Affairs Administration.

Garbage

For complaints about collections, see Sanitation, Dep't. of.

Gas and Electricity, Bureau of

2322 Municipal Building, N.Y., N.Y. 10007.

Highways, Dep't. of

General information, Office of Community Involvement, 566-3680, 566-3644-5-6, 566-3664.

Permits for banners, benches, bicycle racks, canopies, paving, planters, trees, etc., Permit Clerk's office at

BRONX: CY 3-9000.
BROOKLYN: 643-7806.
MANHATTAN: 566-2006-7.
QUEENS: 258-5000.
RICHMOND: 390-5152.

Advice about and permits for structural changes, apply at

BRONX: 851 Grand Concourse, Bronx, N.Y. 10451, Room 101, 566-5777.

BROOKLYN: Municipal Building, Bklyn., N.Y. 11201, Room 1005, 643-4240.

MANHATTAN: Municipal Building, N.Y., N.Y. 10007, Room 1828, 566-2010.

QUEENS: 125-55 Queens Blvd., Kew Gardens, N.Y. 11424, 268-5000 extension 222.

RICHMOND: 100 Borough Hall, Staten Island, N.Y. 10301, Room 25, 390-5152.

Horticultural Society of New York

128 West 58th St., N.Y., N.Y. 10019, 757-0195.

Hoses, use of

For permits to use a hose on buildings, streets or growing things: Dep't. of Water Resources, 566-3344.

Hydrants

Complaints about pressure, disrepair, etc.: Department of Water Resources, 966-7500.

For spray caps: Community Relations Office of your local police station.

Lampposts

For permits to attach anything to lampposts: Dep't. of Public Works, 2322 Municipal Building, N.Y., N.Y. 10007.

Lighting

DECORATIVE
For permits for decorative lighting for festivals, holidays, etc.: Dep't. of Commerce and Industry, PL 9-7770 extension 2425-6.

ON PRIVATE PROPERTY
Lighting for buildings, stoops, gardens, etc., must be done by licensed electrician. For advice: Bureau of Gas and Electricity or Parks Council.

TRAFFIC
For maintenance and repair: Dep't. of Traffic, 361-8000 extension 291.

STREET
Report non-functioning street lights at

Bronx, Manhattan and Richmond: Broadway Maintenance Corp., ST 6-3700.

Brooklyn and Queens: Welsbach Corp., AS 4-4200.

Litter baskets

Dep't. of Sanitation, 125 Worth St., N.Y., N.Y. 10013, Room 823, 566-5442.

Application forms for the placing of special litter baskets should be addressed to the department at the address above, allowing two weeks. Or contact Parks Council.

Lots, vacant

For cleanups: Dep't. of Sanitation, 566-5221.

To determine the owner: Dep't. of Real Estate, 2 Lafayette St., N.Y., N.Y. 10007. Write, giving location of lot and enclosing stamped, self-addressed envelope.

For assistance and educational material in developing city-owned lots: Mayor's Office of Neighborhood Government, 51 Chambers St., N.Y., N.Y. 10007, 566-3600. See also Playlots Project.

Privately owned lots: Parks Council.

Murals

City Walls, Inc., 25 Central Park West, N.Y., N.Y. 10023, 541-8423.

Neighborhood Government, Mayor's Office of

51 Chambers St., N.Y., N.Y. 10007, 566-3600. For advice and assistance on administrative decentralization, block associations, neighborhood action, playlots and play streets.

Noise pollution

See Environmental Protection Administration.

Operation Better Block

For advice on forming and running a neighborhood block association: Mayor's Office of Neighborhood Government, 566-1550.

PAL (Police Athletic League)

For play streets in areas where there are not enough

funds for equipment or supervisory personnel. 34 1/2 12th St., N.Y., N.Y. 10003, OR 7-1400.

Parks Council

80 Central Park West, N.Y., N.Y. 10023, 799-6000.

Parks Recreation and Cultural Affairs Administration

For information, assistance, complaints and permits to plant trees or install planters, contact Department of Parks at

BRONX: Bronx Park East and Birchall Ave., Bronx, N.Y. 10460.
BROOKLYN: Litchfield Mansion, Prospect Park West and 5th St., Bklyn., N.Y. 11215.
MANHATTAN: The Arsenal, 830 5th Ave. at 64th St., N.Y., N.Y. 10021.
QUEENS: The Overlook, Union Tpke. and Park Lane, Kew Gardens, N.Y. 11415.
RICHMOND: Field House, 1150 Clove Rd., at Victory Blvd., Clove Lakes Park, West New Brighton, S.I., N.Y. 10301.

Pavement

For repairs and construction, see Highways, Dep't. of.

Paving

For permits to lay new, block-funded paving: Highways, Dept. of.

Permits

Art work on city building or properties: see Art Commission, City.
Art works on the street: see Art Works on the Street.
Banners: see Banners.
Barbecues: see Barbecues on the Street.
Benches: see Highways, Dep't. of.
Bicycle racks: see Highways, Dep't. of.
Bocci courts: see Bocci.
Canopies: see Highways, Dep't of.
Fairs and Festivals: see Fairs and Festivals.
Fund-raising at street fairs: see Fairs and Festivals.
Furnishings: see Highways, Dep't. of.
Hoses: see Hoses, use of.
Lampposts: for attaching things to them, see Lampposts.
Lighting: see Lighting.
Paving, special: see Highways, Dep't. of.
Planters: see Planters.
Plants: see Plants, Planters and Trees.
Public Address Systems: see Sound.
Scaffolding: see Scaffolding.
Sidewalks, widening: see Sidewalks.

Sound systems: see Sound.
Trees, planting: see Parks, Recreation and Cultural Affairs Administration.

Planters

For permits to install: Dep't. of Highways and Parks, Recreation and Cultural Affairs Administration.

For information: Parks Council.

Plants

For information on selection, planting, installation and care, see Botanic Gardens and Horticultural Society of New York. Also, Parks, Recreation and Cultural Affairs Administration. Also, contact local nurseries.

Annual source of free plants and flowers for community gardens is Wall Street Flower Show, held in April. Write to Parks Council before March 15th.

Play lots

See Lots, vacant.

Play streets

See Neighborhood Government, Mayor's Office on, or PAL.

Police

Dial 911 for emergencies. See your local station house for other matters.

Police Athletic Leagues

See PAL.

Pollution

See Environmental Protection Administration.

Potholes

For complaints: WO 4-2110.

Pools, swimming (portable)

To find out about availability: 533-5031.

Public Arts Council

25 Central Park West, N.Y., N.Y. 10023, 541-8423.

Public Address systems

See Sound.

Public Works, Dep't. of

Municipal building, N.Y., N.Y. 10007, 566-4446.

Recycling depots

For general information: Environmental Action Coalition. Centers open on first Saturday of the month, 10 a.m. to 3 p.m.

Coca Cola Bottling Co.

BROOKLYN: 1900 Linden Blvd., Bklyn., N.Y. 11207, 649-7063.
MANHATTAN: 415 East 34th St., N.Y., N.Y. 10016.
RICHMOND: 2252 Forest Ave., S.I., N.Y. 10303, 447-6224.

Reynolds Aluminum

BRONX: 3960 Merritt Ave., Bronx, N.Y. 10466, 994-5470. (open Saturdays 10 a.m. to 4 p.m.)
BROOKLYN: 341 Nassau Ave., Bklyn., N.Y. 11222, 397-8400.

Refuse

For bulk pickups, see Cleanups.

For inspections: Dep't. of Sanitation, 651-2000.

Salute to the Seasons Fund for a More Beautiful New York

101 Park Ave., N.Y., N.Y. 10016, 689-3374.

Sanitation, Dep't. of

For complaints, requests or assistance: 964-1800.

Scaffolding

For permits to place over sidewalks: Dep't. of Buildings, 566-3941 or 566-4648.

Sewers

For complaints about backups: Environmental Protection Administration, Department of Water Resources, 966-7500.

Sidewalks

For information and advice about, and permits for widening: Dep't. of Highways, 566-3681.

Snow or ice removal

See Sanitation, Dep't. of.

Sound

For permits to use public address systems or other sound devices on the street: Police Dep't., 325 Hudson St., N.Y., N.Y. 10013, 255-1700.

Streets

For complaints about potholes, cave-ins, lane markings or other disrepair: Dep't. of Highways at

BRONX: 293-9000 extension 711.
BROOKLYN: 643-7447.
MANHATTAN: 566-3223-4.
QUEENS: 268-5000 extension 311.
RICHMOND: 390-5142.

Street lights

See lighting, street. Also, Gas and Electricity, Bureau of.

Subsurface utilities

Gas, electric and steam

BRONX: 579-1481.
BROOKLYN: 460-4600. (also Bklyn. Union Gas Co., 643-4275).
MANHATTAN: 576-3216 or 576-2440.
QUEENS: 670-6341.
RICHMOND: 643-4275.

Water Mains: 227-1400.

Sewers: see maps in your local Borough Hall.

Traffic, Dep't. of

For information on parking and traffic, traffic surveys, play streets, signal lights, etc.: 28-11 Bridge Plaza North, Long Island City, Queens, 11101, 361-8000.

Traffic lights

See lighting, traffic.

Traffic Signs

For maintenance and repair complaints: 361-8000 extension 291.

Transportation Administration

40 Worth St., N.Y., N.Y. 10013, 566-3681.

Trees

For permits to plant, advice and complaints on infesta-

tion: Parks, Recreation and Cultural Affairs Administration.
For information on selection and care: Parks Council.

For information on and applications for tree-matching program, write to Parks, Recreation and Cultural Affairs Administration Tree Matching Program, Administration Building, Corona, Queens, 11368.

For general information: Botanic Gardens or Horticultural Society of New York.

Urban Action Task Force
566-1560.

Utilities
For complaints and information

Brooklyn Union Gas Co., 643-4050.

Consolidated Edison Co.

BRONX: 220-2200.
BROOKLYN: 896-5700.
MANHATTAN: 260-3000 (for gas leaks, 683-8830).

QUEENS: 896-6300 (for gas leaks, 670-6285).
RICHMOND: 727-4600.

Long Island Lighting Co., 516 747-1000.

Vacant lots
See lots, vacant.

Water pollution
See Environmental Protection Administration.

Water Resources, Dep't. of
2454 Municipal Building, N.Y., N.Y. 10007, 566-3485.

Weather
933-1212.

Photo credits

Architectural Fiberglass, Inc.: page 44
Berkley, Sheila: page 44
City Walls, Inc.: page 41
Eisenberg, Janie: page 63
Fiori , Clem: cover, page ii, vi, vii, x, 4, 7, 8, 9, 10, 11, 12, 14, 15, 17, 19, 21, 22, 24, 25, 29, 30, 34, 37, 43, 47, 55, 56, 59, 62, 63, 64, 67, 73, 74, 78
Holt, Norma: page 40
Kramer, John: page 3
NBC TV Network: page viii, ix (center bottom)
N.Y.C. Transportation Admin.: page 44
New York Times Inc., The: page 16, 29, 33, 35, 38, 49, 68
Project Two, Stamford, Conn.: page 1
Sullivan, Ed.: page 26
Tapper, David: page ix (left, center top, right)
Timberform, Inc.: page 53